Schirmer's Library of Musical Classics

Vol. 1398

SCOTCH PHANTASY

FOR

VIOLIN AND PIANO

By

MAX BRUCH

Opus 46

Edited by

EFREM ZIMBALIST

ISBN 0-7935-5132-3

G. SCHIRMER, Inc.

DISTRIBUTED BY

HAL•LEONARD®
CORPORATION

7777 W. BLUEMOUND RD. P.O. BOX 13819 MILWAUKEE, WI 53213

Scotch Phantasy

**Edited by
Efrem Zimbalist**

Max Bruch. Op. **46**

I

Andante cantabile (♩ = 88)

attacca

III

Andante sostenuto (♩ = 66)

Più animato (♩= 76)

IV

FINALE
Allegro guerriero (♩=100)

Un poco tranquillo

Scotch Phantasy

Edited by
Efrem Zimbalist

Violin

Max Bruch. Op. 46

INTRODUZIONE

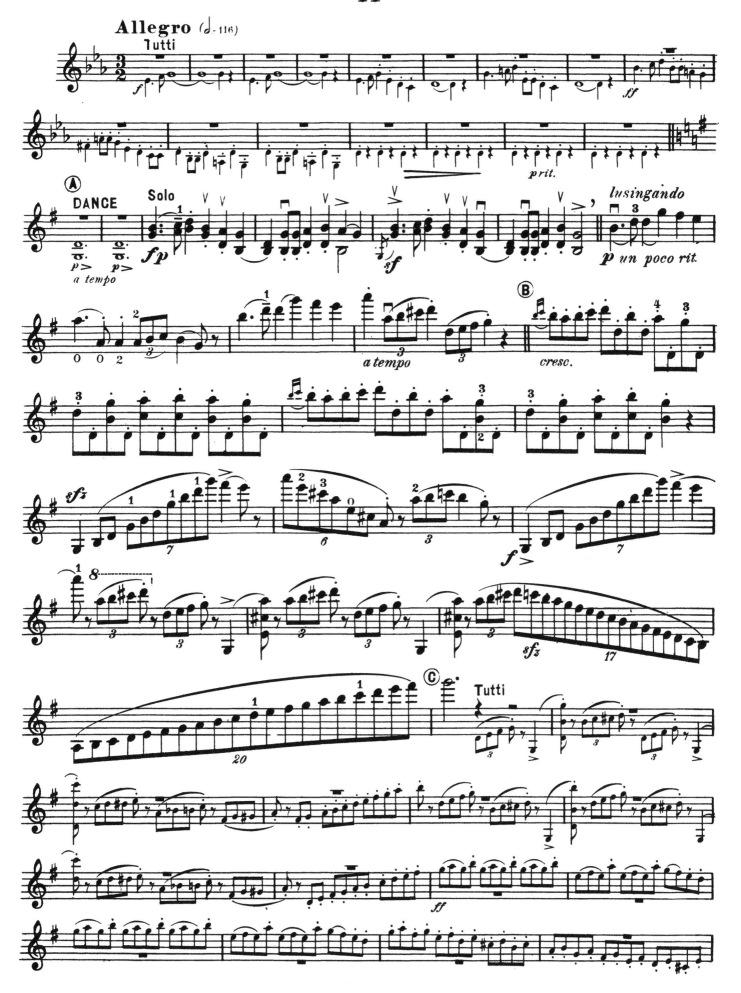

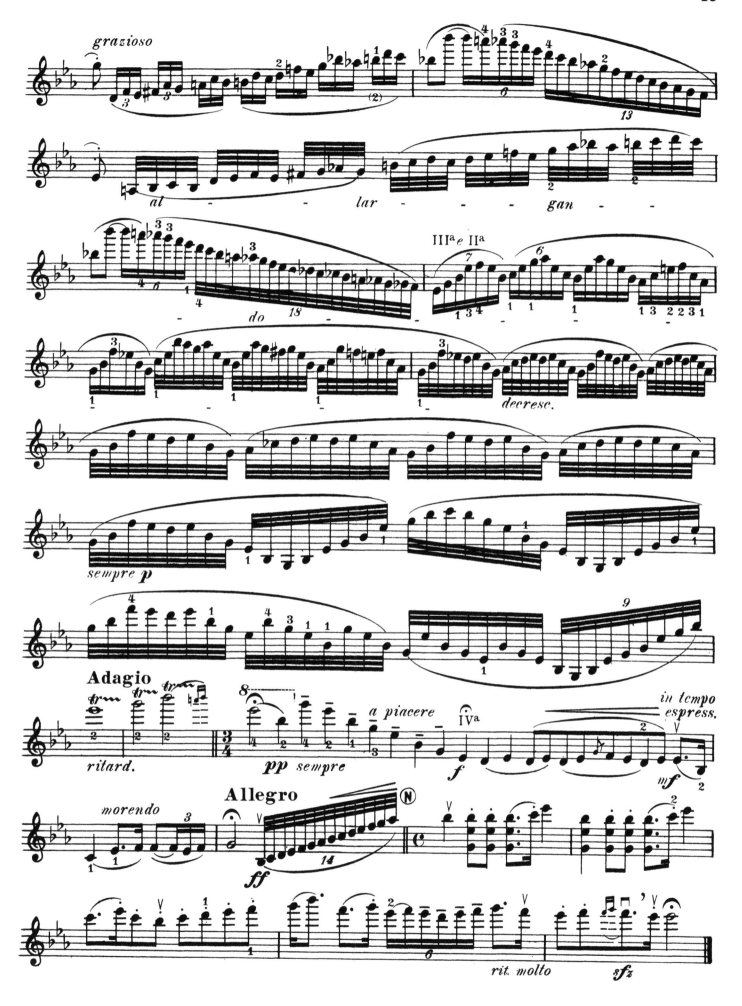